Donald Trump
The Quantum President

by Theeffin Glibrarian

And just because I use sciency words, don't think I
know anything about Sceince. See? I even spelled it
wrong to prove I don't. But *spelling* would actually
fall under Language Arts, so I guess I don't know
anything about that. And using *spellcheck* would come
under Computers, so I don't know those either.

Donald

Trump

The

Quantum

President

This is Donald
J. Trump.

He is both
president and
not-president.

Is that
confusing?

Probably.

So let me
explain.

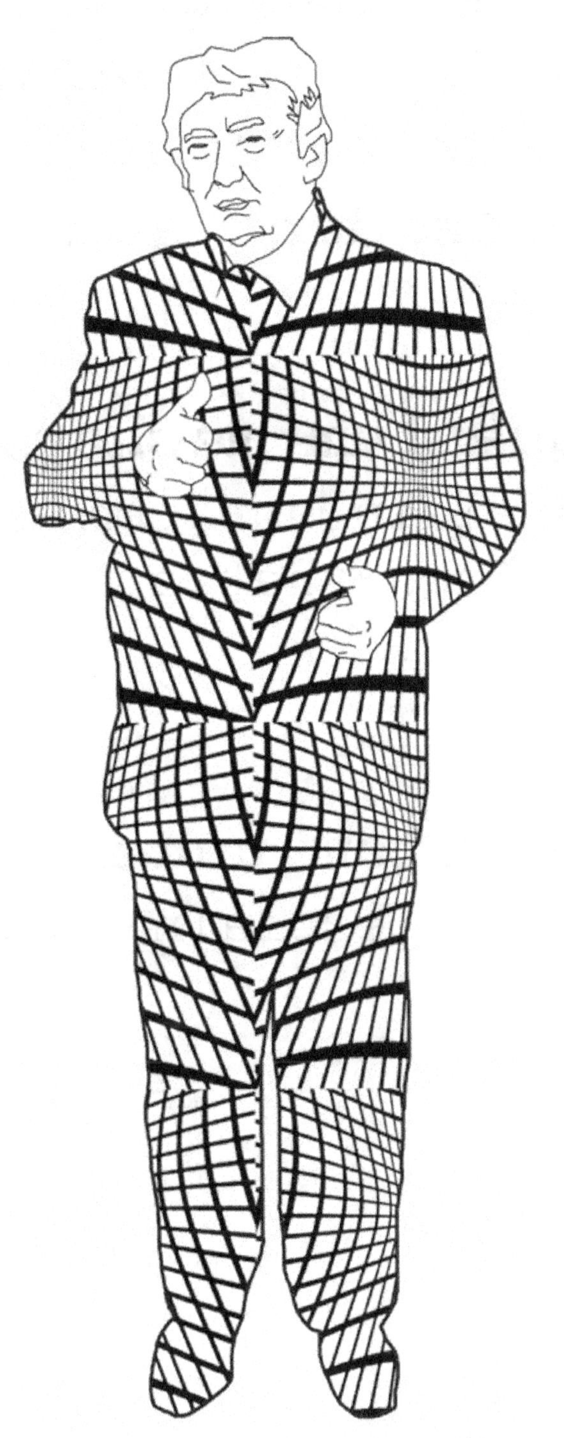

Observing laws of Quantum Mechanics, **Donald Trump is simultaneously both president and not-president.**

Quantum mechanics attempts to explain subatomic particles, things that are smaller than atoms.

Quantum uncertainty is why we can't explain them well.

On a related subject, **one can never know** both the exact location of one of these minute objects and its momentum.

Donald Trump exists as president of The United States of America when he is observed performing his duties presidentially.

Yet, he is **not**-president of The United States of America when he is **in motion and not under direct observation**.

Under observation, Donald Trump's path appears to exhibit predictability. He approaches a decision, claims to support a particular position, and the **probability** that he will continue to support that position is very high.

But no sooner than he moves from our field of view, he changes direction.

So we can never know both his

exact position

and his

current momentum

through observation.

It is during these times when he goes "off script" that he is not-president.

Quantum Mechanics attempts to explain very tiny things that cannot be observed without altering their behavior. **They are so small that even light energy affects them.**

It has been said that Donald Trump's ego is such a tiny thing that each moment influences him from one belief to another.

Many people have said that. People I respect.

Imagine
Trump is
beach ball
floating
in the

Donald
          like a

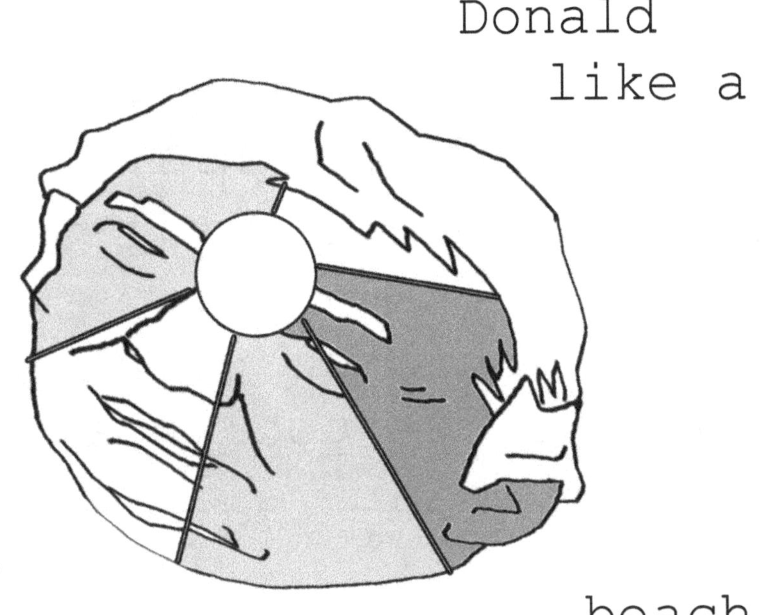

swimming
pool behind
your second
house. The small

                                    beach
                                    beach

house.

Where is the ball at any given
moment?

Who knows?

If the wind is still, the ball could be in the center of the pool, **motionless**, waiting for a breeze to direct its course.

Or it could be clinging to the edge of the pool near the intake filter. Where all the sucking happens.

If the water is **rough**, it might bob around in the waves, traveling around the entire perimeter of the pool.

If Trump meets with **bankers,**
then he thinks **banks** need to be
saved.

If he   meets
with   **gun**

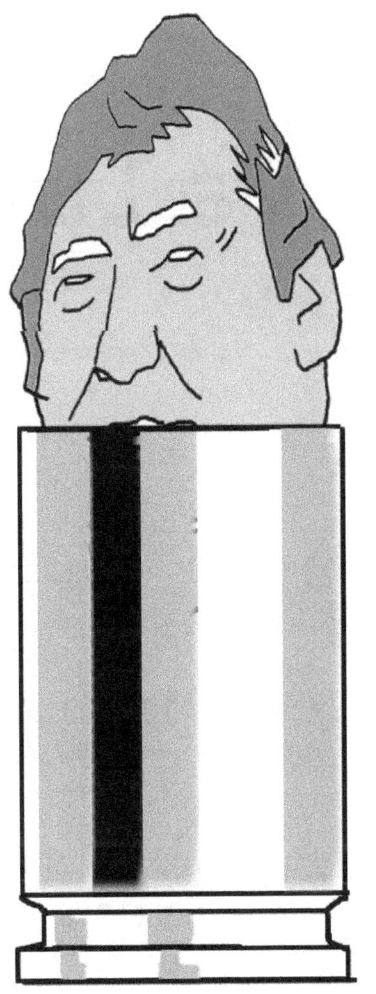

lobbyists, then **guns** and the
gun industry become very
important.

Because of this behavior, he has
no core values. He is liquid. He
is gas. And then he's liquid
again.

He is Value Fluid.

In that case, he could have been
both the beach ball and the
waves in the swimming pool.

Indeed. Donald Trump may be found
to behave as both a particle and
as a wave.

This could explain much.

When it comes to flying around in
Air Force One, he is the
president.

When the country suffers from
multiple incidents of **mass
shooters** who murder American
citizens, and then the survivors
of these attacks and others

cry out for a solution to
stop this bloodshed, he is not
the president.

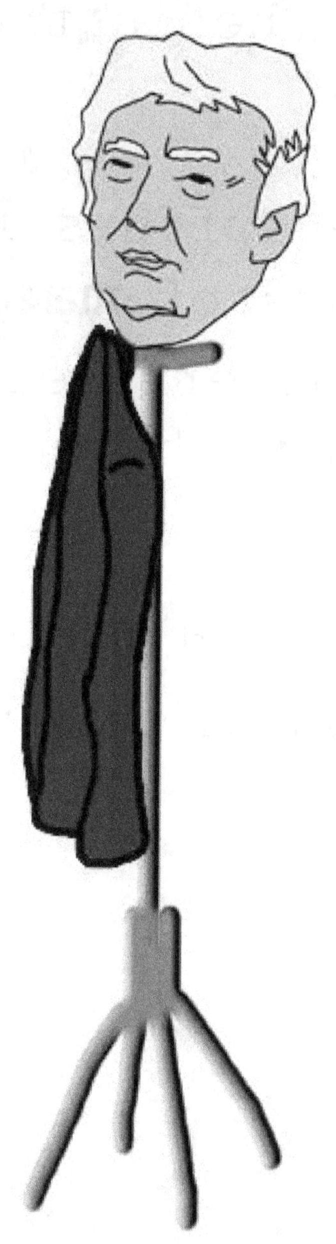

Coat Rack Trump.

Read his tweets and you might
feel his message to us is this:

"Remember that I never wanted to
be the president. I was elected
in spite of all the **terrible
horrible disgusting** things
I've done.

"I tried hard to not be elected.
I even gave very stupid answers
during the Presidential Debates.

"Remember how I didn't know what
the 'nuclear triad' was?

"I said, 'I think for me nuclear
– the power, the devastation is
very important to me,'[1] which is
totally true."

"I love nuclear weapons.

I want to blow up all my enemies.

"But I don't understand nuclear weapons. I think they are big bombs that explode and kill your enemies and then stop killing. I don't understand 'radioactive fallout' because it doesn't concern me.

"In the event of a nuclear attack, some very brave people will put me in a helicopter and take me to a safe place where I will survive just fine. So I don't need to understand radiation."

Donald Trump is lucky. He doesn't need to understand nuclear radiation. Because he will be **president** while he's on that helicopter; yet, **not-president** while he gives a thumbs-up out the helicopter window as nuclear explosions obliterate the people and nation he was elected to protect.

How can one predict that Donald Trump would give a **thumbs-up** as the country is destroyed?

Because someone might be taking his photo.

If you

that
while
are
photos,

have
documents
need signing
reporters
taking
he is the
president.

If **you**
from
at the
those
protect
our

suffer
injustice
hands of
sworn to
you, he is
not-
president.

Thermometer Trump.

If a military parade makes you feel **patriotic**, he is your president.

If you need reassurance and support, **he is not that person**.

Trump l'Orange.

If you love **golf** and have **$200,000** to join his private golf club, he is your president.

If you need a president to make decisions about the welfare of this country that don't involve his **private** business agreements with foreign nations, he is not president.

When it comes to provoking our
enemies, he is here.
When it comes to angering our
allies, he is here, too.[2]

When it comes to building
relationships with world leaders,
we don't know where he is.

And looking for him just makes it worse.

So we wait for him to be
president again.

We wait.

We wait for him to sit in the cab
of a big
truck and
give the
world a
thumbs-up.[3]

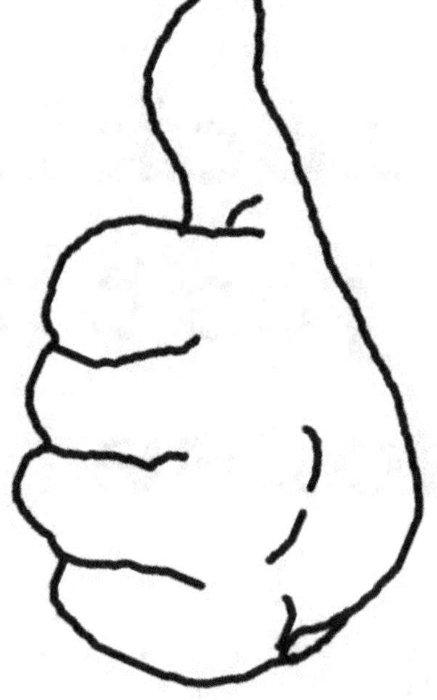

Because that is when he is our
president.

We wonder if that's all he is qualified to handle. We wonder if he's incompetent.

But then the issue is clear. Donald Trump is in a perpetual state of **quantum flux**.

We view his orderly exit from Air Force One, his respectful posture, his salute to Service men and women, and we have a glimpse of someone who could be the president.

But then we witness his somewhat confused glower at the world around him as if he ordered the Porterhouse steak well-done and the server brought him a dog turd, medium. And we remember.

When a woman was killed and it
was clear who was to blame to
everyone but him, he was our not-
president.[4]

When children were murdered in
their classrooms and he ignored
the millions of Americans who
called for action, he was not the
president.

When he posed for a photo with
doctors who treated the
survivors, he wasn't the
president, either.

And when he said he would have
stopped the killer, you could see
that he thought that made him
look like the president. But it
didn't. **Not even close.**

When Americans argue that Donald Trump is

#notmypresident,

they need to understand the science that guides their opinion.

If they want to see Donald Trump acting as our president, then they need to stare directly, forcefully and unblinkingly at him.

And even then, they may never see him. But they may see evidence that he's been seen.

Out of our view, **his position is unknown**. But under focused scrutiny, he may find a way to use his penmanship and photographer-attracting skills to benefit the Country.

And if that doesn't work, being under our constant watchful eyes, just might keep him from blowing up the planet and reducing the rest of us into infinitesimal subatomic particles.

But all this probably won't stop
him from doing

                other

                        stupid

                                things.

References, but clearly there could be more:

1. https://www.rollingstone.com/politics/news/trump
   s-terrifying-nuke-answer-at-the-debate-should-
   end-his-campaign-but-it-wont-20151216
2. https://www.yahoo.com/news/trump-angers-britain-
   midst-london-attack-152524195.html
   or just search for the words, Trump angers
   Sweden, France, Australia, etc.
3. http://www.nydailynews.com/news/national/trump-
   pretends-drive-big-rig-truck-healthcare-bill-
   stalls-article-1.3007134
4. https://www.cnn.com/2017/08/14/politics/charlott
   esville-nazi-trump-statement-trnd/index.html